Kingdom of Shalom Books

YAHWEH

The best things have often been hidden.

Because I will publish the name of יהוה *YHWH:*
ascribe ye greatness unto our God.
Deuteronomy 32:3

YAHWEH

Kingdom of Shalom Books

Discover
Seek
Get To Know

©2023 KOS Publishing
All rights reserved. This book or parts thereof may not be reproduced, scanned, or distributed in print, electronic, stored in any retrieval system, or transmitted in any form by any means—electronic, mechanical, photocopy, recording, or otherwise—without prior written permission of the Publisher, except as provided by United States of America copyright law.

Please purchase only authorized print and electronic editions. Do not distribute, participate in, or encourage piracy of copyrighted material. For permission requests, write to the Publisher at "Attention: Permissions Coordinator" at the email address below.

KOS Books
KOS Publishing
www.kingdomofshalom.com
info@kingofshalom.com

Your support of the author's rights is appreciated.
Yahweh, Book 1
Printed in the United States of America
ISBN 9798989609406 (Hardcover Version)
eBook Version Available on Website

Editorial: KOS Editorial Team
Editing: Olivia Jayden
Cover images: Adobe
Cover Design: Tyron Roshantha
Dedication image design: Cre8tive Minds
Layout: Md Mosarof Hossain

TABLE OF CONTENTS

THE STORY BEHIND THIS BOOK iv
KINGDOM OF SHALOM WORKS v
DEDICATION vi
PREFACE vii
Introduction 1
Chapter 1 7
Chapter 2 13
Chapter 3 17
Chapter 4 21
Chapter 5 25
Chapter 6 31
Chapter 7 35
Chapter 8 40
Chapter 9 45
Chapter 10 51
Chapter 11 55
Chapter 12 75
Closing 79
REFERENCE 83

THE STORY BEHIND THIS BOOK

The story behind this book is simple: to publish the Name of God. The goal of the concept was to share the Name with the world. This book reveals and provides information on the Name, its history, definitions, worshippers, evidence, and significance.

KINGDOM OF SHALOM WORKS

The Kingdom of Shalom emerged from a pursuit to inspire and support those on a spiritual journey and a desire for moral actions to speak louder than words. It is evolving into the Great Work that יהוה YHWH (Yahweh) called for it to become. It is proof that when יהוה **YHWH (Yahweh)** calls, you must answer.

As an organization, we are driven by spiritual ideas, bold actions, and a strong moral foundation of support. We are bringing the Spiritual (the Kingdom of Heaven) down into the minds and hearts of the people.

"Behold, I will do a new thing; now it shall spring forth; shall ye not know it? I will even make a way in the wilderness, and rivers in the desert."
Isaiah 43:19 KJV

Visit the Kingdom of Shalom for more information and other works from KOS Books, Designs, and Publishing.

www.kingdomofshalom.com

DEDICATION

This book is dedicated to the spiritual resurrection of
the righteous people of the Earth, the release and construct
of Spirit and Truth, and the complete establishment
of the Kingdom of God, יהוה **(YHWH) YAHWEH**
--- The Kingdom of Shalom. ---

PREFACE

To receive the whole brevity of the information in this book, you are tasked with lifting your complete self, the mind and body, from the grave where you have been buried. The minds of today are buried 6 feet deep under the 6000 years of dirt (untruths) that have veiled them. These same falsities plagued our ancestors' minds for thousands of years. Even when we think we have some grasp on knowledge, along comes greater wisdom that defeats the beliefs we have walked in and thought we knew.

Get Wisdom and Get Understanding

It is time to consider, become conscious, and create awareness. It is time to engage and challenge all you have known with new insight, comprehension, and adeptness. It is time to awaken by casting the light of truth into the dark places which have plagued us with sleep for far too long.

Therefore, as you raise your mind out of the miry clay, let's look deeper into some myths, fairy tales, fabrications, half-truths, and disinformation to see them all for what they truly are --deception. Trickery has caused your mind to depart and turn away from all TRUTHs.

This Book Is for Renewal.

INTRODUCTION

What if you woke up one day to discover everything about your life had been distorted, changed, made up, or concealed? None of it was real. You found yourself living in a real modern-day -- Truman Show, where your reality was created by someone else, and all you thought you knew was pretend. However, like the movie, you don't realize the world as you know it was unreal.

You had built a life from this imaginary world. You normalized this world and assimilated to its standards, and it had become the mental, physical, emotional, and social norm guiding your thinking and all you do. Then suddenly, there was a glitch in the matrix of your mind. A small ripple of information in the waters of your thinking affected you so much that it became a giant splashing puddle of concepts and knowledge. Its splashing droplets woke you up, causing you to suddenly see things differently.

Suddenly, enlightenment caused you to open your sleeping eyes for the first time to see that the world as you know it was a show. It was created to entertain. This entertainment was not the minds of others but to **enter** and **taint** your mind with unconscious deception and misinformation.

You then find out that you are not alone. This has been going on historically for centuries. This deceit was burrowed into the minds of most of the people you know – family, friends, neighbors, co-workers, and associates- who all accepted this deception as their reality.

What Would You Do?

Deception can be rooted so deeply that even once discovered, most people will consciously decide to return to the deceit they know and continue to walk in the ways of darkness. They do not want to know the truth. They cannot handle the truth. They dislike the feeling of thinking they have been deceived. They do not want to accept any truth that shows they have been deceived. They do not want to acknowledge anything that will disrupt the lives they have built. Even if they find new concepts, if these concepts challenge their belief systems at all, they choose to do nothing. They ignore the new information. Instead of researching the information more, they close the door of their minds. They see no one else is questioning things, so they do not want to make waves. Therefore, they make a conscious decision to go back to sleep and live in an unconscious mental state. They chose an unconscious, unaware, dead state instead of waking up, investigating, and entering a marvelous new light.

Ageless wisdom, sages, wise minds, priests, philosophers, and such all teach that most minds range among those considered the masses, the unenlightened. Even with the advent of information available everywhere, most people choose to watch the show instead of freeing themselves to see what is causing it. Any new light or information hurts their eyes, and they don't want the pain of uneasiness and fear that come with altering one's mind, beliefs, and self.

This thought coincides with concepts such as the Allegory of the Caves. It is worth the short read if you have never read this allegory. An 'allegory' is a concept used to imply something else. Allegories are like metaphors in that both illustrate an idea by making a comparison to something else. However, allegories are complete stories with characters, while metaphors are brief figures of speech. Allegories are a way to convey a bigger message about society or human nature through a straightforward narrative, where various characters may represent real-life individuals. Sometimes, situations in the story may echo stories from history or modern-day life without ever explicitly stating this connection.

In the Allegory of the Cave, there is a cave where people have been imprisoned since childhood. These prisoners can only face forward. They are chained, can't move left or right, and their heads are secured, forcing them to gaze at the wall in front of them. They cannot look around the cave or at each other. Behind the prisoners is a fire, and between the fire and the prisoners, there is a raised walkway with a low wall.

The people walk behind the wall carrying puppets and other living things. The prisoners do not see the people, and the people do not see the prisoners. As the people cross, their bodies do not cast shadows for the prisoners to see, but the objects they carry hang down to cast shadows on the walls facing them. The prisoners cannot see any of what is happening behind them. They can only see the shadows on the cave wall before them. As the people crossing the walkway talk, the sounds echo off the walls, and the prisoners believe these sounds come from the shadows.

The shadows are the reality for the prisoners because they have seen nothing else. They do not realize that they only see shadows of objects dangling in front of a fire, not the actual objects. The shadows are the real things to them. They assimilate to this reality and create their lives with things as they know it. Therefore, they name the shadows, calling them "a book, a tree, a house, a man, etc." They do not know what "a book, a tree, a house, a man" really are in the real world. They are doomed to believe only what they know, which is what they see. Their bondage and the shadows on the wall are their reality. They have no idea that the real world exists outside the cave.

The story then says if one prisoner could free themselves. Then, the freed prisoner could look around and see the fire. But the light from the fire would hurt his eyes and make it difficult for him to see the objects casting the shadows. If he were told that what he saw was real, called fire, and that the shadows were not real, just casts of objects hanging down carried by real people. That this was reality instead of what he thought, the shadows he saw on the wall. He would not believe it. In his pain from the light, the freed prisoner would turn away and run back to look at the wall his mind was accustomed to with the shadows. The light, new knowledge, would hurt his eyes – his mind, and he would escape by turning to the things that he could comprehend. Although he has been exposed to a higher understanding of reality, he wants to remain in his old way of thinking. He chooses the shadowy falseness instead of the new reality being shown to him.

The story continues with, suppose someone dragged him by force up the rough, steep ascent of the cave and never stopped until they dragged him out into the sun's light. The prisoner would be angry and in pain from being dragged up the rough and harsh terrain of the cave. He would kick and scream to not leave the cave, which would only worsen with the sun's radiant light. The Sun represents absolute truth. Since his mind is only conditioned to the darkness, ignorance, and lack of knowledge of the cave, the bright light of truth is agonizing to his eyes – his mind. The sunlight would overwhelm him. It would be painful to his eyes and blind him, meaning it hurts him to see the truth for the first time.

However, out of the cave, his eyes would slowly adjust to the sun's light. First, he could only see shadows. Gradually, he could see the reflections of people and things in the water. Later, he would see people, houses, real objects, and things themselves. Eventually, he could look at the stars and moon at night. Until finally, he could look upon the sun itself. Only after he can look straight at the sun can he understand it, and he becomes overjoyed. As he learns more about this marvelous light, this truth, he is in awe and exhilarated by what he knows.

As he learns more, the freed prisoner sees that the world outside the cave is superior to the world he experienced in the cave. He would bless himself for the change. Then, have pity the other prisoners, desiring to share this world with those who remained in the cave.

Hoping to bring his fellow cave dwellers out of the cave and into the sunlight. He rushes back inside the cave to tell the others about what lies beyond the cave. However, now the returning prisoner, whose eyes have become accustomed to the sunlight, would be blinded by the darkness of the cave when he re-entered. Just as it was when he was first exposed to the sun, he now cannot see in the darkness. When the prisoners who remained in the cave saw the returning man stumbling in blindness, they would become afraid. Not understanding that it was blindness from his eyes not being adjusted to the dark, they would think that the journey out of the cave had harmed him and that they should not undertake a similar journey. When the freed prisoner attempts to tell them about how wonderful life is outside the cave, they laugh at him, thinking he is insane. In fact, they would even try to kill him for daring to tell them they were wrong about what they believed was the truth: the shadows on the wall. The story concludes with if they were able, the prisoners would reach out and kill anyone who attempted to drag them out of the cave into a new reality- new thoughts.

In this allegory, the cave depicts the ignorance of most human beings, chained by their limitations of staring at shadows passing on the wall of their cave minds. The shadows or images on the cave wall constantly change, offering no stability or consistency for those who bear witness to them—only a false reality. People have no knowledge that the real world exists outside of their dark cave thinking and limited beliefs. They do not understand that there is truth other than their beliefs. As the only knowledge one can or is willing to obtain, the cave is deceitful and illegitimate.

Meanwhile, those who escape and leave the cave can no longer exist as they once did in darkness. They want more knowledge. They thirst for it. Eventually, they may even come to pity or feel superior to those who remain in the cave.

The allegory shows the conflicts between knowledge and belief and what happens to a person once they become enlightened. It examines the nature of humanity and the fear of the unknown. The author of the allegory states that people must follow the highest of all studies: To Behold the Good. However, those who ascend to this highest level must not remain there. They have a responsibility to return and help others.

In this book, you will discover information, concepts, and knowledge that may be unknown and completely new. The journey of discovering יהוה YHWH (Yahweh) is an awakening, never-ending escapade filled with a recurring multitude of new bits of intelligence.

A closed mouth and a closed mind do not get fed. For spiritual illumination to penetrate and feed your mind, you must free your mind from the cave's darkness and become an open vessel by seeking the words of truth, studying, and researching new information in search of its truthfulness. Through diligent inquiry, your mind's eye slowly adjusts toward the sun's light. You comprehend **"Let There Be Light"** and know this is where divine wisdom and understanding are found.

May this book be a flame that continues to ignite you out of darkness
and May the End of Your Journey
BE LIGHT!

Chazaq ve'Amatz
(cha-ZAHK veh-eh-MATS)
Be Strong and of Good Courage

Peace and Blessings

Chapter 1

The Mind of Man

Let this mind be in you, which was also in Christ Jesus:
~ Philippians 2:5

Thoughts and ideas begin with the mind. Today, with the constant flow of information and feedback through television, media, sports, social media, and other channels, life generally seems to overwhelm the mind. It is causing people to lose focus and live with ever-going distractions. Overall, these things are changing behaviors and thinking. The pattern of being consistently fed and engrossed in mediums such as those mentioned above agitates the mind and causes chemical changes in our bodies. "You are what you eat!" This is physical food and mental foods, what you put into your mind. They affect and overtake your logical thinking, decision-making, and rational abilities. The evolution of man's mind is an ever-increasing phenomenon or experience, and the need to comprehend the activity of the mind is becoming even more prevalent.

Man's mind is marvelous. It can be used as a magnificently wonderful or an enormously dangerous resource. A mind's destinies lie with what it is connected to, the things or people it bonds with, the networks (how it is programmed), and the relationships it makes. The gift of the mind is that it can change at any time, go another way, or make a different choice. It can choose to be magnificently wonderful or enormously dangerous. The ability to choose either destiny is often called free will.

The Corporeal Mind

When connected to and bonded strictly with worldly knowledge, the mind becomes carnal, secular, terrestrial, and dry, fully gathering and accepting information without full awareness of how the knowledge came to be, nor whether it has truth in it or completely lacks truth.

A mind which receives worldly knowledge alone becomes corporeal. A corporeal mind is material or physical. If material, the mind is filled with delusions of grandeur for material things. It has no regard for anything other than the attainment of material wealth. Materialism is its nature; therefore, one with this mindset sees, seeks, and comprehends based on material possessions. The material mind considers material possessions and physical comfort more important than mental or spiritual values. This mindset is prodigal, wasteful, and fixed on their possessions and the possessions of others. It reigns among the carnal.

A corporeal mind can also be a physical one. If physical, then it pertains to the passions and appetites of the flesh. This is a carnal mind dominated by selfishness. The physical mind is self-willed, stubborn, hardheaded, stiff-necked, self-focused, selfish, or self-seeking. Sometimes, one can have a few or all these attributes. In relationships, this mindset exercises false dominance and forced will over others without regard for anyone except themselves. They will befriend or build relationships based on external appearances. They have little or nothing within, so they look for that in others. They are external seers looking for beauty based on appearances for themselves and with others.

Another type of physical mind is one stuck in a low area of thinking - like a cave. It does not see and does not wish to see higher wisdom. Even when everything around the person fails and falls, those with this mindset look outside themselves to blame others. They refuse to look into the mirror and call for change within, for higher answers.

The material and the physical are carnal minds that have various characteristics. The above are just a few examples. These minds adhere to a sense-driven worldly knowledge. They are low or base states of mind. Such minds are neither mental nor spiritual. They are looped in body awareness, physical realities, and external consciousness. Even having heard higher knowledge, the carnal mind thinks and acts similar to the way it always has, making no changes. It lives according to the senses, more attuned to and concerned about the things of the world. Divine Knowledge and the spiritual realities hardly get these minds' attention. The carnal mind is devoid of the ability to surrender wholeheartedly to Higher Knowledge. They challenge knowledge without prior familiarity. They are not learned or studied, nor do they consider. They see, believe, think, feel, and understand only what they can see on the wall of shadow in front of them: information passed down, given, or told to them.

The Incorporeal

However, a mind open to and connected even a little to spirituality becomes an apparatus for mental and spiritual potency. Led by gaining an understanding of spirit and truth, these minds possess the ability to mutate and transform into something more than their seeded forms. They push towards transpersonal growth beyond the worldly persona and the ego towards a more advanced and evolved mind and self.

The mental or intellectual mind is one with the ability to think and understand ideas and information. It is the faculty of the mind to know and reason. This mind can reach correct conclusions about what is true and false if it seeks reality. The mental mind is smart, knowledgeable, articulate, and curious. One can teach this type of mind to become agile with a growth conviction. As it grows, it will become a mind of true wisdom. If it allows higher knowledge to take hold, it will attain control over their ego and mind's desires. The intellectual mind possesses the ability to gain superior powers of intelligence. It can become highly educated, interested in complicated ideas, and enjoy studying and careful thinking. Through studying, it will become somewhat enlightened. However, it must still become spiritually illuminated to reach its full potential.

Spiritual Illumination

Spiritual Illumination is the emboldening light emanating from the words of Divine Truth, which kindles and activates your mind and heart. It is a spiritual encounter of Divine understanding manifesting within, causing a pouring or downloading of euphoric knowledge beyond mere words. It is a quickening vital spark that revitalizes, invigorates, and wakes your mind and body by shining, radiant. Divine Light filters into the dim, dark areas of your being, bringing you into an internal and external new celestial existence. Spiritual Illumination creates a spiritual mind.

The spiritual mind is a fully resurrected mind and soul that has emerged from the cave of darkness. It is awake and aware, realizes and understands Divine Knowledge, connects with it, holds on to it, and will not let go. It is a mind parked on spiritual things, filled with holy desires, higher sacred knowledge, and divine purpose. Spirit has illuminated it. Therefore, it emanates the marvelous light of the Divine. This mind comprehends that although intellectual knowledge raises the mind, only through the power of the Divine Life Force can one become and know they are spiritual. With this new illumination of spiritual wisdom, one with this mindset realizes all things are possible because spirit is in all things and the answer for all things.

Chapter
2

Spirit

"And the Spirit of God moved upon the face of the waters."
~ Genesis 1:2 KJV

Let us begin with the Spirit. Everything and all things are Spirit. You may already know this, or you might not. So, I will repeat. Everything is Spirit.

We are made of spirit, soul, mind, and body. These four elements make up the whole self. They are one in you, me, and everyone else. Over our lifetimes, we live in the physical, focusing primarily on material things. These are those things that we can see, touch, hear, taste, and smell, all the things that stimulate the physical senses somehow. We focus so much on the physical that we forget, learn very little, or never learn about our minds, souls, or the spiritual part of ourselves. Only recently have we found and learned some mental things from a psychological or behavioral view. But even with this, we learn nothing about the soul or spirit, even though all these and again everything is spirit.

Even religious institutions do not teach the form and wisdom of spirit. What is known is only shadows. Without understanding the spirit, soul, and mind, you are left with the life stories of physical knowledge with no inner meaning. Learning about your spirit, how it affects your life, or how to be one with spirit is the step to unbinding and freeing your mind, soul, and body. Being without the knowledge of spirit has left a catastrophic hole in people's lives since life itself is spirit, soul, and mind, linked together with the body. The three missing elements form and play major roles in the story of ourselves.

Often, Spirit is called Energy. The things we learn about spirit are reclassified into the word energy. We learn in science that all things are made of energy. However, if everything is spirit, are spirit and energy the same? The answer to this lies in the definition of spirit. There is spiritual energy, but there is also mental and physical energy. There are various forces that make up the spiritual and mental realms which are not and cannot be classified by science. However, they do exist, and Consciousness, as in the Universal Conscious, is the interactive interface between them.

Energy is defined as the ability to do **work.** Another word related to energy is 'power.' Throughout the history of different cultures, people have often used the words 'energy' and **'power'** to describe their experience of God, gods, or other spiritual forces. Some ancient cultures, as well as contemporary cultures, identify God's being with supernatural energy itself.

In higher forms of thinking, energy represents the Ener-G, Inner God, or Spirit. Here, all definitions of energy fall in line with this thinking. A root word of energy from Greek *energeia* is "activity, action, operation." Biblically, the same word in the New Testament is used only when speaking of works or workings - Superhuman Power, such as Spirit, God, or Miraculous Works they cannot phantom. Energeia is pronounced - En-erg'-i-ah. The '-iah' is another word for Yah or Yahweh. The 'en' means 'in, inside, within,' and the 'erg' means 'work, works, workings.' Therefore, Energy - Energeia – (En-erg-iah) means the inner workings of God, Yahweh, Yahweh works within, or the works of Yahweh are within. This confirms *Luke 17:21... "behold, the kingdom of God is within you."*

Awakening

The true definition of "awakening" or being "woke" is becoming conscious of the Spirit or your spiritual self. Defined, "Spirit is the invisible, indestructible life force in everything. It is the energy or working function of all activities. The one and only energy, absolute and neutral, broken up and distributed throughout the universe and more." Therefore, Spirit is found everywhere, in the inanimate and animate. Spirit exists in our nervous system, body structures, and the bloodstream. It is considered an absolute necessity for life in humans. It is the vital life force in all beings and living things.

Spirit is also the inward intuitive direction guiding an individual through life. This is important for you to consider because you may not realize that a "still small voice" is guiding you within. But there is, and it is called spirit. Other definitions say spiritual is attitudinal growth, gaining a new understanding, progressing, and evolving into information that leads to higher intelligence and wisdom. This is inner growth and understanding of the spiritual aspects of things, most importantly, yourself.

Spirituality is gaining an understanding of the intrinsic nature and quality of things. It is about learning the essence of everything we see, hear, smell, taste, and touch. However, learning the essence of a thing is distinct from its physical form or what it looks like. Essence goes into higher understandings. It is seeking to understand the nature of a thing. It is learning the true latent force or characteristic within a thing. This force or feature is within all things and desires to manifest to a bigger ideal than itself. Meaning it wants to be known. Thus, spirituality and becoming spiritual is to grow in mental awareness and attitude.

The true meaning of spirit probably lies within and without these definitions' limits. Spirit is one of those higher forms of wisdom outside of the limited level of a definition or the "cave knowledge." It should not be limited to the shadowed meaning. Therefore, understanding spirit beyond words means it must be sought out and experienced.

Chapter
3

GOD

"And God spake all these words, saying, I am the יהוה YHWH thy God, which have brought thee out of the land of Egypt, out of the house of bondage. Thou shalt have no other gods before me."
~Exodus 20:1-3

God: the creator and ruler of the universe and source of all moral authority; the supreme being. In certain other religions, a superhuman being or spirit is worshiped as having power over nature or human fortunes. God is a deity.

- **God** – "God," with its capitalization, respectfully acknowledges that there is only one true 'God.' It does not name him with his proper Name, Yahweh. The personal Name of God is Yahweh. It is a foreign name, quite un-English, unlike the good Anglo-Saxon word 'God.'

God is the supreme or ultimate reality. He is considered a being perfect in power, wisdom, and goodness. The term God is worshipped in modern Judaism, Christianity, Islam, and Hinduism and is seen as the creator and ruler of the universe. Christian theologians taught that God created the universe throughout the patristic and medieval periods.

The concept of God is highly complex and varies greatly depending on one's religious, philosophical, and cultural beliefs. Different religions and belief systems have their understandings of God or gods, and there are also atheistic and agnostic perspectives that do not affirm the existence of a deity. Here are a few common perspectives on the concept of God:

Religions

Monotheistic Religions: In monotheistic religions such as Christianity, Islam, and Judaism, God is typically understood as a singular, all-powerful, and all-knowing being who created the universe and continues to govern it. These religions often emphasize the qualities of omnipotence, omniscience, omnipresence, and benevolence.

In Christianity, God is believed to be the eternal, supreme being who created and preserves all things. Christians believe in a monotheistic conception of God, which is both transcendent (wholly independent of and removed from the material universe) and immanent (involved in the material universe).

Polytheistic Religions: Unlike monotheism, polytheistic religions like Hinduism and ancient Greek or Roman mythology involve belief in multiple gods and goddesses, each with their own powers and domains. These gods are often associated with various aspects of life and nature.

Pantheism: Pantheism holds that God is synonymous with the universe itself. In this view, everything in the universe is divine, and there is no distinction between God and the natural world. Some notable pantheists include the philosopher Baruch Spinoza and some interpretations of Eastern religions like Taoism.

Deism: Deism is a belief that a divine creator sets the universe in motion but does not actively intervene in human affairs. Deists often see God as a distant and non-personal entity.

Atheism: Atheism is the belief that there is no God or gods. Atheists reject the existence of a deity and often seek naturalistic explanations for the origins and workings of the universe.

Agnosticism: Agnosticism is a position that neither affirms nor denies the existence of God. Agnostics argue that the existence of God is unknowable or that there is insufficient evidence to make a definitive judgment.

It's important to recognize that discussions about God can be deeply personal and are shaped by individual beliefs, cultural backgrounds, and personal experiences. The concept of God remains a philosophical and theological debate, and people's understanding of God can be highly nuanced and diverse.

In religious and philosophical discussions, the idea of God as the creator of the universe refers to the belief that God is responsible for bringing everything into existence. It suggests that God is the ultimate source from which all that exists originated. This concept is particularly important in monotheistic religions like Christianity, Islam, and Judaism.

Here's a simplified explanation:

God is seen as the divine force or being that made everything in the world. It's the idea that God caused the universe and everything in it to come into being, essentially making the world as we know it. This understanding emphasizes that nothing in the universe would exist without God's creative act.

Chapter
4

Who Is Yahweh

"And Moses said unto God, Behold, when I come unto the children of Israel, and shall say unto them, The God of your fathers hath sent me unto you; and they shall say to me, What is his name? what shall I say unto them?"
~Exodus 3:13 KJV

WHO IS YAHWEH?

When this question is asked, one of the first definitions you may find is,

"Yahweh, the name for the God of the Israelites, representing the biblical pronunciation of "YHWH," the Hebrew Name revealed to Moses in the book of Exodus." ~ Encyclopedia Britannica - Yahweh

Others say *Yahweh is the Name of the state god of the ancient Kingdom of Israel and, later, the Kingdom of Judah.* ~World History Encyclopedia - Yahweh

Or you may come across, *"Yahweh was an ancient Levantine deity and national god of the Israelite kingdoms of Israel and Judah."* ~ Wikipedia - Yahweh

While these and other statements hold truth, they do not even come close to the - who, what, nor who is not or what is not Yahweh.

יהוה YHWH (YAHWEH)

יהוה **YHWH (YAHWEH)** is the Name of the God of the Bible. Strictly speaking, Yahweh is the only "true" Name of God. "Yahweh" is the Hebrew word, the self-revealed Name of the God of the Old Testament and the God spoken of in the Bible.

This is a fact that is true for any religion that uses the King James Version or any Hebrew or English translations of the Hebrew or Greek Scrolls. The God spoken of in these texts is יהוה **YHWH (YAHWEH)**.

The name יהוה **YHWH (YAHWEH)** first appears in the Bible in Genesis 2:4. ***"These are the generations of the heavens and of the earth when they were created, in the day that the LORD God made the earth and the heavens,)."*** Here in the Hebrew translation of this verse, *the LORD* is – the tetragrammaton יהוה **YHWH (Yahweh).**

It's important to note that the historical and linguistic origins of "Yahweh" are subject to scholarly debate and research. The Name is believed to have ancient Semitic roots. It is a proper name linked to the Hebrew verb and root "hayah, (היה)," which means "be, to exist, become, come to pass." However, the Name's exact etymology and historical development are unknown.

The name "יהוה **YHWH (YAHWEH)**" is profoundly significant in the Hebrew Scriptures, called the Old Testament, and is central to the Israelites' practices, beliefs, and complete way of life. "יהוה **YHWH (YAHWEH)**" is often associated with omnipotence, omniscience, and holiness. It is linked to the idea of a personal God who is all-powerful, knows all, is involved in the lives of humans, and has a covenantal relationship with the people of Israel.

יהוה **YHWH (YAHWEH)** is the personal Name of the God of the Abrahamic beliefs and religions. The Name, יהוה **YHWH (YAHWEH)**, was considered so sacred by some that they never casually spoke it, as in the modern Jewish religion today. Instead, alternative names or titles are used instead of the proper Name.

YAHWEH IS SPIRIT

Everything is made of spirit. Therefore, everything is made with and of Yahweh.

*God, יהוה **YHWH (YAHWEH)**, is a Spirit: and they that worship him must worship him in spirit and in truth. ~John 4:24 KJV*

It is impossible to worship God, יהוה **YHWH (YAHWEH),** without understanding the truth of יהוה **YHWH (YAHWEH).** The truth frees you from a dark and unknowing mind to a receptive one.

"And ye shall know the truth, and the truth shall make you free." ~John 8:32 KJV.

The truth does not change. The sun rises in the East, and it sets in the West. This is an example of truth. This statement about the sun is the same truth today as yesterday. It will also be the same tomorrow. The truth remains past, present, and future.

Truth is consistent with fact. It is something real, genuine, not counterfeit or fake. Truth is accurate and correct. Truth is also defined as a covenant or pledge. It causes one to be firm, solid in beliefs, steadfast, and unwavering because it is backed with real information. Therefore, the one with the truth becomes faithful and exercises fidelity and loyalty.

Truth must be implanted in your head. It is a must that you study the information you are told in search of the truth. When the truth is found, studying is necessary for information to go from seed to root. Once opened with this freedom that is gained from the truth about God, יהוה **YHWH (YAHWEH),** you are ready to receive the wisdom of spirit, Spiritual Illumination, in your heart.

For I am יהוה YHWH, I change not; therefore, ye sons of Jacob are not consumed. ~Malachi 3:6 KJV

Chapter
5

Yahweh, Known Before the Hebrews

"I am Alpha and Omega, the beginning and the ending, saith יהוה YHWH, which is, and which was, and which is to come, the Almighty."
~ Revelation 1:8 KJV

───────────────

The name "יהוה YHWH (Yahweh)" is specifically associated with the God of the Hebrew Scriptures. יהוה YHWH (Yahweh), as God, has historical origins rooted in the Hebrew Scriptures (the Old Testament) and the traditions of the Israelites. The use of the Name and its development are primarily associated with the Hebrew people. "Yahweh" has long been linked to the narrative of God's self-revelation to Moses in the Book of Exodus, where God identifies Himself as "I AM WHO I AM" (Exodus 3:14). This Divine Name was communicated to Moses as a way of revealing God's nature and character to the Israelites.

While some historical connections between the name "Yahweh" and other ancient Semitic cultures have been proposed by scholars, the Name is most commonly associated with the Hebrew tradition and the Israelites and their spiritual understanding of the God of Abraham, Isaac, and Jacob. This connection with the Israelites begins with the encounter between Moses and Yahweh in Exodus 3:14 KJV – *"And God said unto Moses, I AM THAT I AM: and he said, Thus shalt thou say unto the children of Israel, I AM hath sent me unto you."* Within the context of the Hebrew Scriptures and the Israelites' spiritual heritage, Yahweh is primary and most significant.

However, according to the Bible, the name יהוה **YHWH (Yahweh)** goes back to the creation of Adam in Genesis Chapter 2:4 KJV.

> *"These are the generations of the heavens and of the earth when they were created, in the day that <u>the LORD</u> God made the earth and the heavens,"*

It is here that the name of God is first introduced. In this scripture, "the LORD" in the concordance is the word Hebrew 3068, יהוה **YHWH**. When you add the name of God back into its rightful place in the Bible, this bible verse now reads,

> *"These are the generations of the heavens and of the earth when they were created, in the day that <u>יהוה</u> **YHWH** God made the earth and the heavens."*

As a matter of fact, in every place where you see the capitalized "LORD" in the Bible, the word LORD is replacing the name יהוה **YHWH**, and this was done almost 7000 times.

For God's name to be presented in one book almost 7,000 times says a lot about its importance. There is much to say on this subject. But, for now, we want to keep the focus on Genesis 2:4 as being the first time יהוה **YHWH's** name is said in the Bible because a few things are shown to us here.

First, this verse tells us the name of the God who create, formed and made the earth and the heavens. It specifically says "יהוה **YHWH**." This same God created everything on the Earth, including Adam. Therefore, it can easily be deduced that יהוה **YHWH** is the God of the earth and all humankind.

Second, this verse shows that the wisdom and understanding of the Name יהוה **YHWH (Yahweh)** was known to the family of Adam. This wisdom and understanding of the Name יהוה **YHWH (Yahweh)** was also known to Cain and Abel as seen in Genesis 4:3-4 KJV,

> *"And in process of time it came to pass, that Cain brought of the fruit of the ground an offering unto יהוה YHWH. And Abel, he also brought of the firstlings of his flock and of the fat thereof. And יהוה YHWH had respect unto Abel and to his offering.*

Here, יהוה **YHWH**'s name is mentioned in the verse dealing with Cain as well as the one dealing with Abel.

Third, something happened after Cain killed Abel. Cain left, and it seems the knowledge of the name יהוה **YHWH (Yahweh)** goes away. The wisdom and understanding of the Name יהוה **YHWH (Yahweh)** was unknown again until Seth's son Enos, according to Genesis 4:26,

> *"And to Seth, to him also there was born a son; and he called his name Enos: then began men to call upon the name of יהוה **YHWH.**"*

Enos was the next to know the name of יהוה YHWH. Enos was a son of Adam's son, Seth. The above Bible verse even says men called upon the name of יהוה **YHWH.** Seth's family line goes to Enos and continues down to Noah.

There are several verses which show that Noah knew and understood the name יהוה **YHWH.** It is said that Noah possibly built the ark in Mesopotamia, modern-day Iraq. If this is true, then some of these people who have known and even at one time worshiped יהוה **YHWH.** This becomes an even greater possibility when considering that Mesopotamia, modern-day Iraq, is also where the "Garden of Eden" was thought to have been. Therefore, it would make sense for some of the generations of Adam, like Noah, to still live in that area.

The ark that Noah built landed in the mountains of Ararat, according to Genesis 8:4. Today, Mount Ararat is located in the Eastern Anatolia Region of Turkey, Armenia. So, the name יהוה **YHWH** continued to spread in this area also, even if only through Noah and his family.

The Chaldeans

Their history spans more than 5,500 years, dating back to Mesopotamia. The Chaldeans were also said to live in southern Babylonia, the land bordering the head of the Persian Gulf between the Arabian desert and the Euphrates. This is where Ur was located. Ur is the place where Abraham was from.

The Ancient Canaanites Also Worshipped יהוה YHWH Yahweh

While the worship of יהוה **YHWH Yahweh** is primarily associated with the ancient Hebrews and their religious practices, some historical and linguistic connections exist between the ancient Hebrews and the Canaanites.

The Canaanites were a diverse group of ancient Semitic people who inhabited the region of Canaan. This includes present-day Israel, Palestine, Lebanon, and parts of Syria and Jordan before the Israelite conquest. They are said to have practiced polytheistic worship with a pantheon of gods and goddesses, such as Baal, El, Asherah, and Yahweh.

The worship of יהוה **YHWH Yahweh** as the sole God and the central focus of monotheistic worship is a unique development within the Hebrew tradition. The Hebrew Scriptures recount the story of the Israelites' interactions with יהוה **YHWH Yahweh**. This includes their Covenant with Him, the giving of the Ten Commandments, and the establishment of religious laws and practices. The worship of יהוה **YHWH Yahweh** included sacrifices, rituals, prayers, and observing festivals and Sabbath days.

The distinction between יהוה **YHWH Yahweh** worship and Canaanite religious practices is clear in biblical narratives that describe conflicts between the Israelites and the worshipers of Canaanite deities. The Hebrew Scriptures often emphasize the importance of worshiping יהוה YHWH Yahweh only and not adopting the practices of neighboring cultures.

Chapter
6

There Is No "J" In Hebrew

"The very greatest is the alphabet, for in it lies the deepest wisdom; yet only he can fathom it, who truly knows how to put it together."
~ EMANUEL GEIBEL

The "J" was one of the last letters to be added to many letter systems or alphabet. The letter "J" was not added to the Bible until the 1629 Cambridge Revised Version. The letter 'J' did not even exist when the Hebrew and Greek sections of the Bible were written.

Studying language evolution and historical phonetics provides valuable insights into how letters and sounds have transformed over time. One intriguing aspect of this evolution is the absence of the letter 'J' in the Hebrew and Greek languages, the languages of the Old and New Testaments in the Bible. This absence has implications for biblical names and their original forms, shedding light on the linguistic history of all the names that begin with 'J,' including Joshua, Judah, Jesus, and Jehovah.

There is no letter "J" in the ancient Hebrew language, not one in modern-day Hebrew, nor has there ever been one. As a result, none of the names of persons, places, or things could have begun with or included the letter 'J.' This is the same as with the Greek language used to write the New Testament. There is no 'J' in the Greek alphabet. The Greek language does not have a symbol for 'J' or a sound equivalent to our 'J' sound.

The letter 'J' was added to the Latin alphabet in the Late Middle Ages. In the Roman alphabet, which is the English alphabet's father, the letter 'J' did not exist. What we know as "J" was a fancier way of writing the letter 'I.' It was called a **swash letter**. This meant the letter we know as 'J' was a more decorative way to write an 'I' with an extended down and curved stroke, like writing calligraphy. There was no sound to it.

Both the 'I' and 'J' were often erroneously used interchangeably by European scribes. However, it wasn't until 1524 that Gian Giorgio Trissino, an Italian Renaissance grammarian, clearly distinguished between the two sounds. The letter J was first distinguished from 'I' by the Frenchman Pierre Ramus around 1559, during the 16th century.

However, "J" did not become common in Modern English until the late 17th century, so early 17th-century works such as the first edition of the King James Version of the Bible (1611) continued to print all names in the Hebrew and Greek Scriptures with the correct corresponding sounds represented by letters or combinations of letters. The Hebrews used a 'Y,' and the Greeks primarily used an 'I.'

The use of 'J' is an error and mistranslation of any Hebrew word that begins with the 'Y.' YHWH reads the same in Hebrew and Greek. Since there is no letter 'J' in the original and current Hebrew alphabets, the first letter, 'Yod,' could have only been transliterated into a 'Y.' Just like there was never a 'J' in the original Hebrew language, there were also no vowels.

The letter 'J' that we know today was the last addition to the English alphabet. Based on this book's publishing date, the letter 'J' is less than or around 500 years old.

Chapter
7

Yahweh Replaced

"And I appeared unto Abraham, unto Isaac, and unto Jacob, by the name of God Almighty, but by my name יהוה YHWH (YAHWEH) was I not known to them."
~Exodus 6:3 KJV

The name יהוה **YHWH (YAHWEH)** was replaced in the Bible. Even when you go to the above scripture, it reads, "but by my Name JEHOVAH was I not known to them. In the Strong's Concordance, this is H3068 (Hebrew word 3068) in the concordance, which is יהוה or YHWH, yet they have used the word Jehovah to replace Yahweh. However, the Brown, Driver, Briggs Lexicon clarifies this error. It says יהוה the proper Name of the Deity, Yahweh, the proper Name of the God of Israel.

The name יהוה **YHWH (YAHWEH)** was revealed in the book of Exodus. It was represented in the Bible and pronounced **"Yahweh."** Before they removed יהוה **YHWH (YAHWEH)** from the Bible, it occurred almost 7000 times in the Hebrew Scriptures.

Why Was the Name יהוה YHWH (YAHWEH) Removed

This tradition of never speaking the Name prompted the Hebrew vowel system to be invented in the Middle Ages. The rabbis who wrote the scriptures added the vowels for Adonai to the Tetragrammaton as a reminder not to say God's true Name out loud. This tradition dates back to the mid-2nd century BC, during the Hellenistic period (c. 332–37 BC).

Today, these replacements have wiped the Name יהוה **YHWH (YAHWEH)** completely out of the Bible. Biblical scholars chose to preserve the true Name and hid it by teaching never to say it. Because of the perceived holiness of God's Name, the Jews and those within the Jewish religion were taught never to utter the Name of יהוה **YHWH (YAHWEH)** aloud. They use *HaShem*, the Hebrew word for **"the name,"** or *Adonai*, the word for **"Lord."** None of today's three most popular English Bible translations contain the proper Name for the God of Israel, Yahweh. The capitalized title 'LORD' replaced 'Yahweh' in the King James Version (KJV) of the Bible, the New American Standard Bible, and the New International Version (NIV).

"Jewish religious leaders introduced the tradition of adding **LORD** and **God** in the mid-2nd century, which has continued since then. This manufactured tradition - which achieved near-universal acceptance in 1611 AD when the King James Bible editors failed to include the name 'Yahweh' in their inaugural edition - is wrong and dangerous for two reasons. First, it nullifies Yahweh's explicit command to tell the world that we have only one God - Yahweh. Second, according to the Bible, Yahweh is the only Name by which we have salvation. That's a startling fact to most Christians because many have never heard a preacher say it from the pulpit, but it is true nonetheless."

~ **His Name Is Yahweh Organization**
HTTP://www.hisnameisyahweh.org

Chapter
8

Many Names and Many Titles

And the great dragon was cast out, that old serpent, called the Devil, and Satan, which deceiveth the whole world: he was cast out into the earth, and his angels were cast out with him.
~Revelation 12:9 KJV

Jehovah, God, Lord, Yahweh Are They All The Same As?

The correct form and pronunciation of the Name of the God of Israel is one of the most challenging mysteries of Biblical scholarship. Even though the name יהוה **YHWH (YAHWEH)** is better known and less hidden, it is often mispronounced or confused with other words.

It is often said that God has many names and titles, but is this true? Or is it true that humans have just given God the names and titles they have chosen to address God with? Let's investigate some of these names and titles to see what we are able to discover.

El, Elohim, El Elyon, El Shaddai, Lord, and Other Titles

- God: In the Hebrew Scriptures, each time you see the word "**God**," it is the Hebrew word Elohim, H430 in the Strong's Concordance. We will look further into the word God in our Chapter entitled "God."

- **Elohim** is the Hebrew word that translates as "Powers: Divine ones – superhuman beings including gods, goddesses, and angels. Rulers and judges as divine representatives at Holy places or as reflecting divine majesty." It is the plural of Eloha.

- Eloha is a deity or the Deity.

- El Elyon means The Power over All Creation.

- El Shaddai - Shaddai is "sufficient," so El Shaddai is the "God almighty, The Almighty, All-sufficient One."

- The word "**Lord or My Lord**" translates to Adonai.

- **HaShem** means "The Name."

- **Amen - Who or what is Amen? Amen** is a name that has survived from very ancient times, going back to the Egyptian pre-historical era. Although many people know Amen as a declaration of affirmation for prayer, which is first found in the Old and New Testaments. Amen was the principal Egyptian state god in the New Kingdom, closely associated with Thebes at least as far back as the Middle Kingdom.

- **EL - "El"** had multiple meanings in the northwestern Semitic language. El is the word for "god," the Name of a specific god, and the title of a god who stands apart from other, lesser gods.

Although many of these titles represent characteristics or aspects of Yahweh, titles are not the same as Yahweh's Name.

Jehovah Did Not Appear Until The 16th Century.

In 1530, William Tyndale was the first to remove Yahweh from the English Bible when he translated the first five books of the Hebrew Bible to English. Tyndale was ignorant of the history of the word "Yahweh." He had no knowledge that the rabbis chose to add the vowels for Adonai onto the Tetragrammaton as a reminder not to say God's true Name out loud. He didn't understand that because of the perceived holiness of God's Name, many Jews never uttered it aloud. Nor did he know they used *HaShem*, the Hebrew word for "**the name,**" or *Adonai*, the word for "**Lord**." Therefore, William Tyndale eventually translated the four-letter Hebrew word 'יהוה **YHWH (YAHWEH)**' into the mistranslated word "Jehovah."

Within his translation of the Bible into English, he included the Name of God, misspelled as *Iehouah*, in several verses. "In the notes section of Tyndale's Bible, he wrote: Iehovah is God's Name…" More importantly, Tyndale changed every area where the Tetragrammaton originally was to the capitalized word "LORD." In the comments section of his translated English versions of the first five books of the Bible, he wrote, ***"Over as oft as thou seest LORD in great letters (except there be any error in the printing) it is in Hebrew Iehovah."*** The meaning of this comment is **["Wherever you see LORD in capital letters (except for errors in the printing), it is in Hebrew - Jehovah"]**.

From this practice by Tyndale, the use of the erroneous translation of Yahweh's Name to Jehovah in just a few verses arose. Then, the replacement later continued by writing "LORD" or "God" in most other places where the Tetragrammaton originated in Hebrew. Tyndale's translations into English ultimately became the basis for the Old Testament of the King James Version of the Bible in 1611, and the rest is history. This mistranslation of the Name Yahweh became the source for all other English translations that followed it.

No matter the evidence shown, some people maintain that יהוה **YHWH (YAHWEH)** Yahweh's Name is Yehovah or Jehovah, which is not true. Again, this form is a hybrid developed by adding the vowel points from the Hebrew word *Adonai*, Lord, to the Tetragrammaton. Those vowels were never intended to be inserted into the Tetragrammaton.

The Name is יהוה YHWH without the added vowels, and when it is translated into English, YHWH becomes Yahweh.

"YAHWEH. The vocalization of the four consonants of the Israelite Name for God, which scholars believe to approximate the original pronunciation."

~The Bible's Interpreter's Dictionary

"Because of its Holy Character, the Name Yahweh was withdrawn from ordinary speech during the Second Temple (c. 500 BCE and later), and the substitute word — actually a title, not a personal name — Adonai, or (The) Lord, was used, as is still the practice in synagogues. Scholars who translated the Hebrew Bible into Greek (the Septuagint) in the third century BCE adopted this synagogue convention and rendered YHWH as (ho) Kurios, '(The) Lord.' The practice was carried over from this Greek translation into the New Testament."

~ Understanding the Old Testament

The pronunciation Jehovah was unknown until 1520, when it was introduced by Galatinus, but was contested by Le Mercier, J. Drusius, and L. Capellus, as against grammatical and historical propriety."

~The New Brown, Driver, and Briggs Hebrew and English Lexicon of the Old Testament

"Jehovah," Vol. 16, p. 8. "An erroneous pronunciation of the name of the God of Israel in the Bible, due to pronouncing the vowels of the term 'Adonay,' the marginal Masoretic reading, with the consonants of the text-reading 'Yahweh'…"

~ Encyclopedia Americana

"The word Jehovah is an artificial form that arose from the erroneous combination of the consonants YHWH with the vowels of Adonai — written under or over the Hebrew consonants to indicate that the substitute is to be pronounced. This hybrid form is often considered the invention of Pater Galatin (a Catholic priest named

Peter Gallatin) ...but actually, it can be traced back to a work by a certain Raymond Martin in 1270."

~ Understanding the Old Testament

"Yahweh - the Covenant God of Israel, YHWH, in the original Hebrew. According to Jewish custom, the Name was not to be spoken because of reverence."

~The King James Version of the Bible by Thomas Nelson, Bible Dictionary

"Jehovah in that form was unknown to the ancient Israelites. Hebrew scholars say that Jehovah would have been impossible according to the strict principles of Hebrew vocalization. The God of Israel was known by a name approximately rendered into English as Yahweh." ~ **A Book About the Bible**

Although the meaning of the Name remains debatable, Yahweh is most likely a verbal form of Heb. *haya* (perhaps originally *hwy*) ...Because of the utmost sanctity ascribed to the Name, Jews from postexilic times on have declined to pronounce it in public reading, and only the consonants were written (YHWH; the Dead Sea Scrolls use the archaic, 'paleo-Hebrew' script). Although the original pronunciation was thus eventually lost, inscriptional evidence favors *yahwae* or *yahwe*.

~The Eerdmans Bible Dictionary

"Yahweh was without doubt the approximate pronunciation of the Tetragrammaton, the four-letter word YHWH, since transliterations into Greek in early Christian literature have been found in the form of *iaoue* (Clement of Alexander) and *iahe* (Theodoret) pronounced *'iave*." ~ **The Journey from Texts to Translations**

Chapter 9

Yahweh In The Abrahamic Religions

"For there is nothing covered, that shall not be revealed; neither hid, that shall not be known. Therefore, whatsoever ye have spoken in darkness shall be heard in the light; and that which ye have spoken in the ear in closets shall be proclaimed upon the housetops."
~Luke 12:2-3.

For thousands of years, the name יהוה **YHWH (Yahweh)** has been the name that represents the Divine Creator in many monotheistic religious traditions. In some religions, יהוה **YHWH (Yahweh)** is a part of their history. In other religions, יהוה **YHWH (Yahweh) is their One God** and the focus of their devotion.

MUSLIMS

In Islam:

While "Yahweh" is not explicitly used in Islamic texts, the Islamic tradition recognizes the Abrahamic God as the same God the Israelites worshipped. Abraham from the Bible is a Hebrew. Genesis 14:13 KJV, **"And there came one that had escaped, and told Abram the Hebrew."**

Abram, whose Name changed to Abraham, had two sons, Isaac and Ishmael. Isaac was the firstborn son and only child of Abraham and his wife, Sarah. According to the Hebrew Scriptures, the Old Testament, Isaac was destined to become the heir of Abraham. Genesis 17:19 KJV, *"And God said, Sarah thy wife shall bear thee a son indeed; and thou shalt call his name Isaac: and I will establish my covenant with him for an everlasting covenant, and with his seed after him."* Isaac is the father of Jacob and one of the three forefathers of the Hebrew Israelites.

Ishmael was the first child of Abraham. In Hebrew, Yishma'el literally means "God hears or to hear and obey God." Ishmael was born from Sarah's Egyptian handmaiden, Hagar when Sarah thought she was barren. As a son of Abraham, Ishmael learned about יהוה **YHWH Yahweh** from his father, Abraham. Genesis teaches that he was sent away and driven into the wilderness with his mother. However, יהוה **YHWH Yahweh** blessed Ishmael also, Genesis 17:20, *"And as for Ishmael, I have heard thee: Behold, I have blessed him, and will make him fruitful, and will multiply him exceedingly; twelve princes shall he beget, and I will make him a great nation."*

Ishmael is important in the Islamic faith. Ishmaelite is a name given to the descendants of Ishmael. "Islam" means "submission to the Will of God." Islam is a religious system revealed by Muhammad. The followers of Islam are called Muslims. Muslims recognize Ishmael as the ancestor of Muhammad.

Ishmael is the forefather of the Islamic faith. Isaac and Ishmael are brothers by blood. Both are the children of Abraham. Therefore, the children of Isaac, the Hebrew Israelites, and Ishmael, the Ishmaelites-Islamic nation, are family and blood relatives.

Muslims are monotheistic and worship one, all-knowing God known as Allah in Arabic. In Islam, the language spoken is Arabic. God is known by the Arabic name "Allah." Etymologically, Allah is possibly a contraction of the Arabic al-Ilāh. It literally means "the God," from *al* or *el* "the" + *Ilah* "God." Allah's origin can be traced to the earliest Semitic writings, whose word for God was **Il, El,** or **Eloah**. The latter two, **El** and **Eloah**, are in the Hebrew scriptures, the Old Testament, as definitions for God. Like Hebrew, Islamic monotheism emphasizes the concept of the Oneness of God.

CATHOLICS AND CHRISTIANS

Catholicism

Catholicism was created during. As a branch of Christianity, Roman Catholicism traces its history to Jesus, Yahshua during Roman-occupied Jewish Palestine in the early 30s CE. His followers spread across many lands for years after Jesus, Yahshua's life and death. The goal was to form a "universal" (Greek, **Katholikos**) church with the bishop of Rome holding primacy.

The Roman Empire was enormous. It spanned over 5 million square miles. There was a struggle for the emperors in Rome to maintain power over the large area. By 330, Emperor Constantine split the empire in two: the Western Roman Empire, in Rome, and the Eastern Roman Empire, or Byzantine Empire, with Constantinople as its new capital. Latin was largely spoken in the west, and Greek in the east. However, the church was still unified for the most part.

What started as geographic, political, and language differences between the Eastern and Western churches began to include differences in theological practices (the study of God) and eschatological beliefs (relating to death, judgment, and the final destiny of the soul and humankind). These differences throughout the years culminated with each side calling the other heretics who were not to be trusted or tolerated.

The Great Schism

In July 1054, Michael Cerularius was excommunicated from the Christian church based in Rome, Italy. His excommunication was a breaking point in the long-rising tensions between the Roman and the Byzantine churches, resulting in a split that divided the European Christian church into two major branches. This split is known as the Great Schism, the Schism of 1054, or sometimes the East-West Schism.

The "Great Schism" created the two largest Christian denominations of the time—the Roman Catholic and Eastern Orthodox faiths. All other Western Christian religious groups, Protestant, Lutheran, and others, arose from these two denominations.

Christianity

Originally, a Christian was a person who worked to have the manner and spiritual character necessary to follow Christ. Today, they are believers in and followers of Christ. They profess the Christian religion and teachings received from the Christian church. Christ is a title given to Jesus of Nazareth. Jesus is from the Greek name Iesous. It means Yahweh is Salvation. Jesus was a Hebrew. The name Jesus, Iesous, was created from the Hebrew name Yahshua or Yehoshua, which has the same meaning. The title Christ comes from the Latin **Christus** and the Greek **Khristos.** It means Anointed One. The word Christ is synonymous with and a translation of the Hebrew word **Mashiach,** which means messiah.

Unlike during ancient Greco-Roman times, modern Christians never directly use the Name יהוה **YHWH (Yahweh)**. However, Christianity, particularly within the context of the Holy Trinity (Father, Son, and Holy Spirit), views Yahweh as the God of the Old Testament and the Creator of all. "Yahweh" is God's Divine identity, including the personification of God the Father. Jesus, Yahshua, was a Hebrew. He believed in, worshipped, and taught about the Hebrew God, יהוה **YHWH (Yahweh)**.

St. John 5:43 KJV, *"I am come in my <u>Father's Name</u>, and ye receive me not: if another shall come in his own name, him ye will receive."* What is the Father's Name? For Jesus, Yahshua, the Hebrew, it was the Hebrew God - יהוה **YHWH (Yahweh)**.

Chapter
10

Hidden and Unspoken

*"Fear them not therefore: for there is nothing covered, that shall not be revealed; and hid, that shall not be known.
~Matthew 10:26 KJV"*

THE HIDDEN NAME

Knowledge of the name "יהוה YHWH (Yahweh)" first appeared in Catholic hymns in the early 1970s. This happened through the influence of The Jerusalem Bible, whose English translation appeared in 1966. In August 2008, US bishops were directed to remove Yahweh from songs and prayers. However, the name יהוה **YHWH (Yahweh)** was known and used within the Catholic and Christian religions long before the 1960s and 1970s.

During the Hellenic history between 800 BC and 500 AD, Greek and ancient Roman historians and archaeologists viewed the public and private rituals associated with religion as part of everyday life. These rituals, examples of phenomena, miracles, or what the Greeks named Magic, are still found in temples, Jewish synagogues, and European churches. These were important hubs for ancient people, representing a connection between the heavenly realms, the Divine and the earthly planes, or the earth.

Also, around this Hellenic time, Jewish rabbis began to stop using the name Yahweh. Their goal was to preserve the name and keep it secret.

Over the years, there have been many religions, groups, organizations, and people who have kept the Name יהוה **YHWH (Yahweh)** a secret from the masses. The Catholic church was one of these, as seen in the 2017 article below.

An article from World News - Real News Right Now

In 2017, Pope Francis Orders Vatican Archives to Reveal God's Name, Ending Centuries of Secrecy

VATICAN CITY – Speaking before a delegation of Jewish leaders at the Vatican on Thursday, Pope Francis revealed he has instructed the Vatican Secret Archives to unseal a set of ancient scrolls that have been kept hidden from public knowledge for centuries by the Church. The scrolls, which were encased in marble and buried in 463 AD, are said to contain the true Name of God as communicated to Moses in the Book of Exodus.

The Pope told an audience during an event celebrating a new version of the Torah that his decision to upend over fifteen hundred years of secrecy was driven in part by a need for "greater transparency" within the Catholic Church. "It is a scandal to say one thing and do another," declared Pope Francis before adding that the Church is "leading a double life" by continuing to keep God's name secret.

A source inside the Vatican Secret Archives told Sky News that the Church first became aware of the scrolls' existence in the fifth century. "The scrolls were uncovered by the Romans during the siege of Jerusalem and the subsequent destruction of the Temple in 70 AD. Nearly four centuries came to pass before Rome would hand over control of the scrolls to the Church in 463 AD," the source explained. "Upon inspection, Pope St. Hilarius issued a decree striking any mention of God's name from official Church literature."

According to Exodus 3:14, when the Lord appeared to Moses as a burning bush, He referred to Himself in the Hebrew tongue as "YAHWEH," meaning, "I am who I am." However, the Holy See now says that was only part of God's message to Moses. "God said, 'I am who I am,'" the Vatican source told Sky News. "He then followed up with, 'And I am [this name].' That final word is what the Holy See plans to make known to the world."

Why the Catholic Church has gone to such great lengths to keep God's true Name a secret remains unknown. What is clear is that the Papacy has maintained an unbroken chain of communication regarding the matter dating back to 468 AD. "In keeping with tradition, each successive Pope since Hilarius has been made aware of the Lord's name," Vatican spokesman Greg Burke confirmed on Friday.

The Vatican Press Office has received more than two million inquiries regarding God's Name since the Pope's announcement on Thursday. "Our phones have been ringing off the hook," said one Vatican insider who spoke to BBC News on condition of anonymity. "Understandably, everyone wants to know [His] name," the insider said. That sentiment isn't limited to the public. Even the College of Cardinals is getting caught up in the frenzy.

~Article **FEBRUARY 24, 2017,** *by R. HOBBUS JD.*

Chapter
11

יהוה Yhwh (Yahweh) Around The World

> *"For the earth shall be filled with the knowledge of the glory of the LORD, as the waters cover the sea."*
> *~Habakkuk 2:14.*

The name יהוה **YHWH (Yahweh)** is known and seen in many lands throughout the world. Often, people don't always recognize or know the Tetragrammaton יהוה YHWH (Yahweh). They are unfamiliar with the ancient or modern Hebrew Characters portraying The Name. Also, because they have been misinformed about the correct transliteration of the Name, those who see it do not realize they are seeing the Name יהוה **YHWH (Yahweh)** in its purest form, the Holy Hebrew.

"The nation of Moab was related to the Israelites. The Moabites were a tribe of people who descended from Moab, one the sons of Lot. Lot was Abraham's nephew, who left his home and went into the desert with Abraham, when Abraham was instructed to leave by God יהוה **YHWH (Yahweh)**. The Moabites were said to be a highly developed culture, with artifacts written in Hebrew bearing Moabite inscriptions. The Moabites are the ancient Semitic civilization that is mentioned in the Moabite Stone, the Mesha Stele."

Whether known or unknown, the Name יהוה **YHWH (Yahweh)** is all over the world.

ENGRAVINGS

One of the oldest known inscriptions of the Tetragrammaton dates to 840 BC. The Mesha Stele bears the earliest known reference, around 840 BC, to the Israelite God יהוה YHWH (Yahweh).

The Moabite Stone, known as the Mesha Stone

Caption: YHWH, the god of Israelites, as mentioned in the Moabite inscription in line 18. The text reads, *"And I took from there the vessels of YHWH, and I dragged them before the face of Kemosh."* Transliteration of modern Hebrew characters: יהוה. Louvre Museum Collect. Photo by Henri Sivonen.

Magic Disc

Caption: Amulet; silver; disc; pierced and engraved. On the obverse is the central motif of the seal of Venus, surrounded by an inscription and a planetary symbol of Venus, the symbol of the intelligence of Venus, and the symbol of Libra. On the reverse is the numerical square of Venus (7x7 rows) in Hebrew letters, surrounded on three sides by Hebrew inscriptions with the Tetragrammaton at the top and the total sum of the numerical square, 1225.

BUILDINGS, DOORS, WINDOWS, ALTARS, CEILINGS

Holmens Kirke Copenhagen - portal north

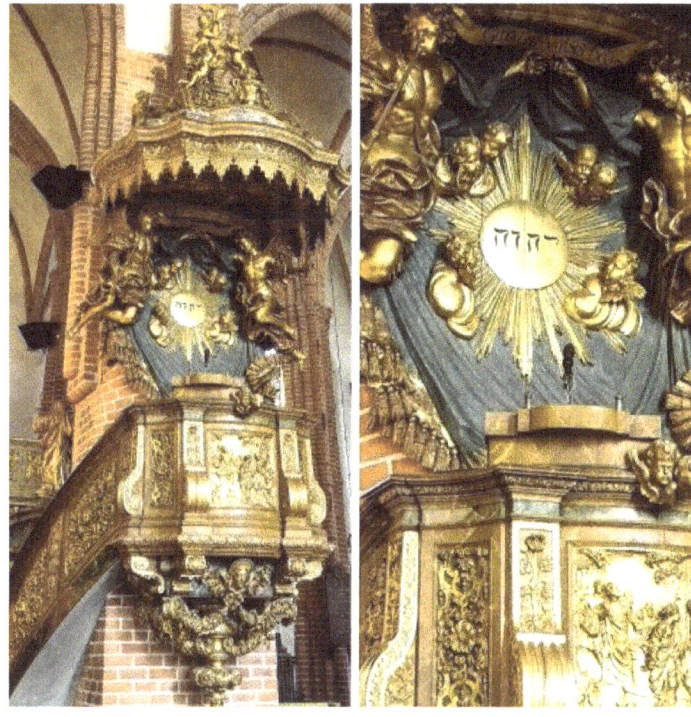

The great church in Stockholm pulpit

Screen of Holstein Chapel in St. Aegidien, Lübeck

The Golden Unicorn Hotel in Prague with Tetragrammaton - Yahweh

ALTARS AND CEILINGS

In Sweden - Svenska Njutångers kyrka- Pulpit with the tetragrammaton YHWH in the sun symbol.

Tetragrammaton (YHWH) on the top at the church of St. Merri at Paris, near the Centre Pompidou

Draschwitz church - Elsteraue, district Burgenlandkreis, Saxony-Anhalt

Sweden - SThe Swedish Pulpit in Barva Church."

Statue located within the Basilica in Rome

Sainte-Croix cathedral, Orleans, Loiret, France, Europe

Built 1834 - Basilica of Saint Louis, King of France located in Saint Louis, Missouri, USA

BUILDINGS AND STATUES

BUILDINGS AND FOUNTAINS

Votivkirche_Tetragrammaton By Niki.L - a protected monument in Austria

Valley Rock Fountain in Scotland - Geograph Photo

Main Entrance, Saint Francis Cathedral, Santa Fe, NM

Parma, Province of Parma, Italy

The Sun Symbol in the pulpit with the Tetragrammaton YHWH in Saint Nicolai Church

Cherubim surround the Tetragrammaton sculpture - the Basilique, Notre Dame des Victoires Paris

Stained glass from the Staind Glass Museum in Chicago

"Main altar with the baroque painting of Saint Michael by Josef Ferdinand Fromiller at the parish church Saints Michael and George, municipality Moosburg, district Klagenfurt Land, Carinthia, Austria. Photo by Johann Jaritz"

Tetragrammaton at Roman Catholic Church Saint-Germain, Paris France

Tetragrammaton in the East Window at St. Mary's Church in Wivenhoe

ANCIENT PRINTS AND ART IN BOOKS

For thousands of years, books have been printed that displayed the Divine name יהוה **YHWH (Yahweh).** The name of god, יהוה **YHWH,** was added to the books to show the sacredness of some of the information within them. Many of these ancient books and art still exist and have been preserved in museums and private collections. These are a few books printed during the 1600s, with covers or inserted art which display the name. They include books on natural history, medicine, surgery, astronomy – the universe.

"The following six book covers and/or inserts are examples of the artwork that displays the name יהוה **YHWH Yahweh**" in their design."

~ All Images from the British Museum - www.britishmuseum.org

1611 PHARAMACOPOEIA LONDINENSIS

Cover to 'Pharmacopoeia Londinensis' (London, John Marriott, 1618); title in the center; above, the royal coat of arms between two obelisks and beneath a cloud inscribed with the Tetragrammaton and from which a hand extends; to the left of the title, Hippocrates, standing, holding a book; to the right of the title, Galen, standing and holding a book; bottom left and right, half-length portraits of Mesue and Avicenna; bottom center, a shield featuring an emblem of two hands clasped above a thistle. Engraving

1630 AN APOLOGIE - DECLARATION OF POWER AND PROVIDENCE OF GOD

An Apologie or Declaration of the Power and Providence of God' (London, Robert Allott, 1630); title in the center, between two Ionic columns at the top, the sun, moon, and stars, with the Tetragrammaton.

1631 SYLVA SYLVARVM OR A NATURALL HISTORIE IN 10 CENTURIES

Sylva sylvarum, or A natural history in ten centuries: together with the History natural and experimental of life and death, or of the prolongation of life: whereunto is added Articles of enquiry touching metals and minerals and the New Atlantis, with an alphabetical table of the principal things contained in the ten centuries.

1633 QUADRIVIUM SIONIS OR THE FOURE WAYS TO SION

"Quadrivium Sionis or the foure ways to Sion" by John Monlas, a renowned work from 1633. The intricate engraving, executed by William Marshall, is a true masterpiece that resides in a private collection. The focal point of this image is undoubtedly the majestic name of God, Yahweh, prominently displayed in Hebrew within the sky.

1639 THE SURGEON'S MATE

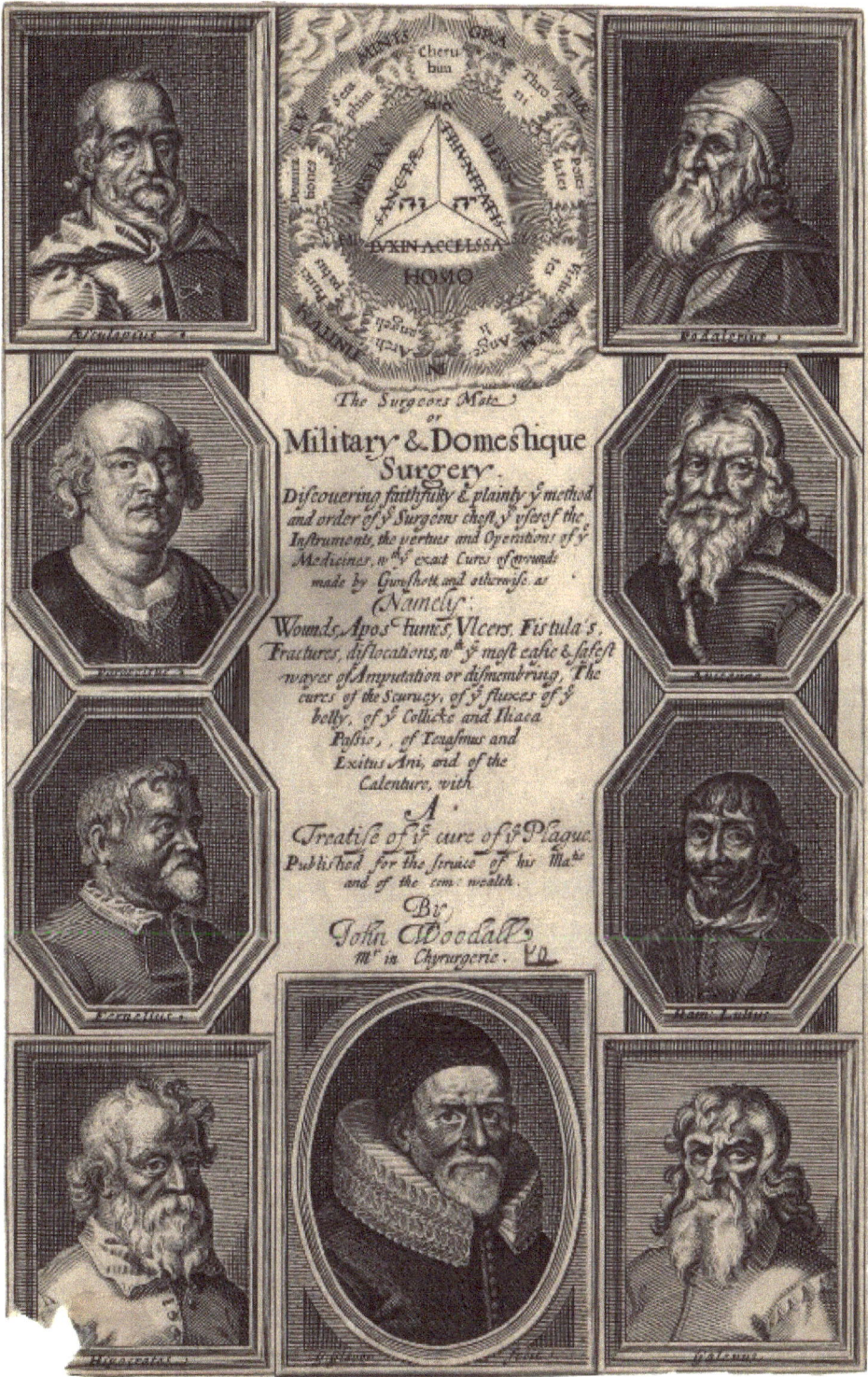

Cover to John Woodall's 'The Surgeons Mate: or Military & Domestique Surgery' (1639); the title in the center, with Tetragrammaton within lettered diagram in a wreath at the top, and a portrait of the author in an oval below, bust, to the right, wearing a skull cap and ruff, with pointed beard; on the left side from top to bottom portraits of Aesculapius, Paracelsus, Gernelius and Hippocrates; and on the right side from top Podalerius, Avicenna, Ram: Lulius, and Galenus. 1639

1666 COSMOGRAPHIE IN FOUR BOOKS

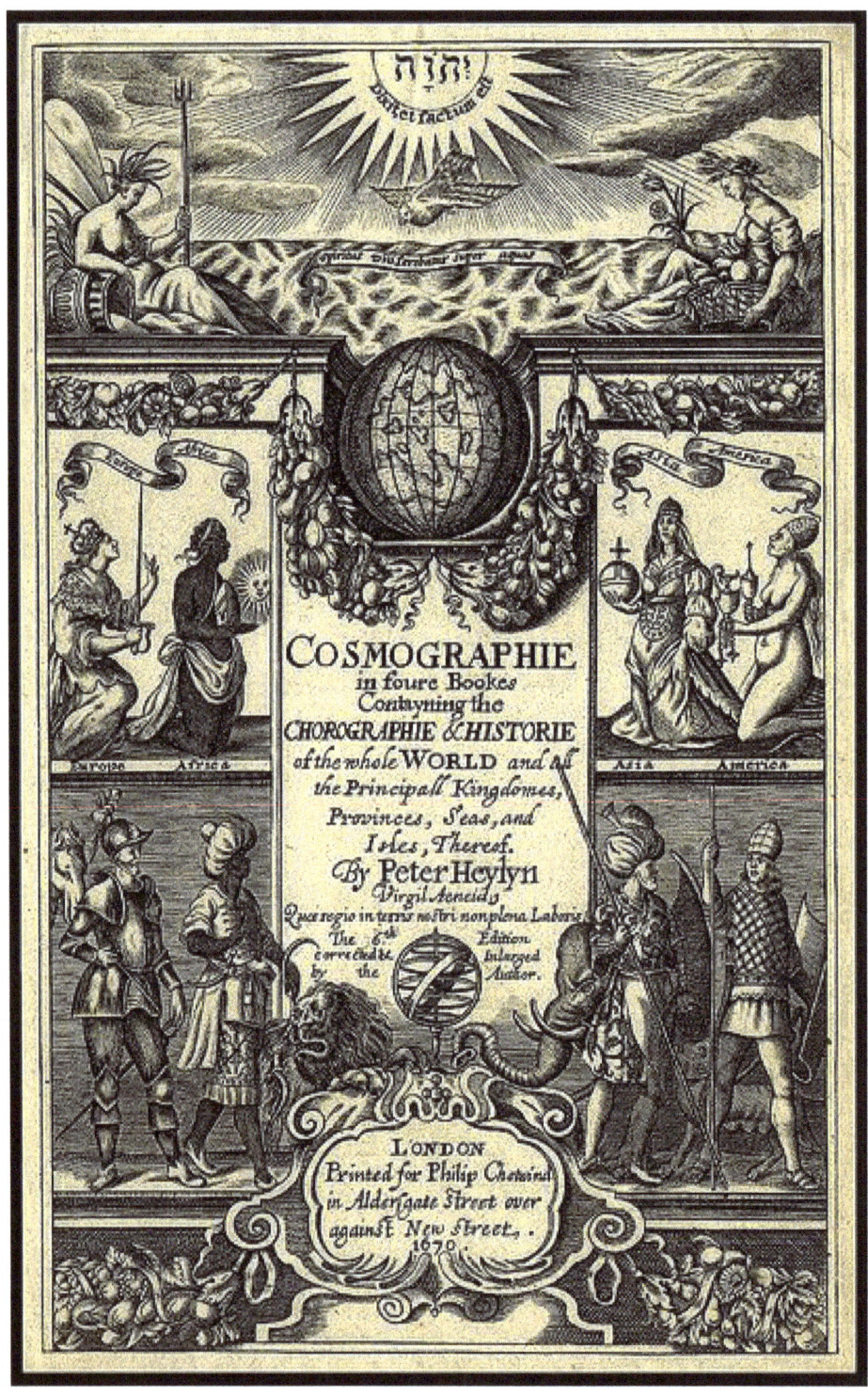

Title-page to Peter Heylyn, 'Cosmographie', 3rd enlarged and corrected edition (London, Philip Chetwind, 1666; first published, 1652); title in the center below swags of fruit hanging from cornice; globe above fruit, and, at the top, the sea, with a dove over the waters and the inscription 'Spiritus Dni ferebatur super aquas'; Tetragrammaton above dove; top left and right, female figures, one with trident and barrel, the other with flower and basket of fruit; center left and right, female figures representing Europe, Africa, Asia, and America, below which corresponding male warriors, with horse, lion, elephant, and dog.

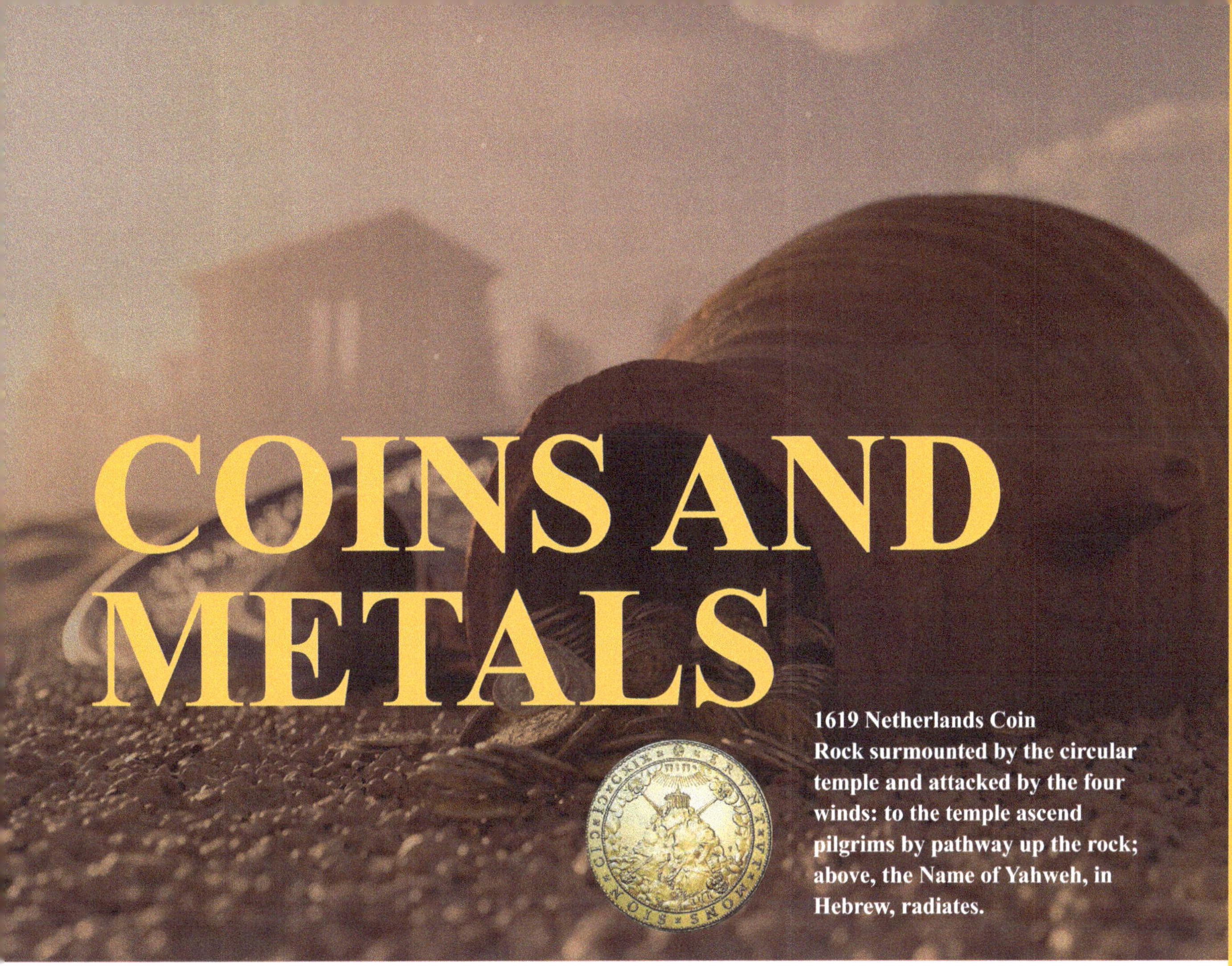

COINS AND METALS

1619 Netherlands Coin
Rock surmounted by the circular temple and attacked by the four winds: to the temple ascend pilgrims by pathway up the rock; above, the Name of Yahweh, in Hebrew, radiates.

1 German States - Hesse-Cassel. Death 2 Ducats, 1637-GK. Fr-1255

During the 1500s, more than 500 years ago, people were very familiar with יהוה **YHWH (Yahweh),** the Name of God. During that time, places like Paris, Sweden, the Netherlands, Scotland, Italy, Vienna, Germany, Austria, and others celebrated and preserved the name יהוה **YHWH (Yahweh)** by placing it everywhere. As

1574 coin Tetragrammaton made in Dordrecht

1588 Anglo-Spanish War THE SPANISH ARMADA

1588 Coin Flavit Yahweh et Dissipati Sunt with the word YHWH in Hebrew letters - means God blew, and they were scattered

1599 Swedish Carl IX Regency Period Daler

1606 Stockholm Carl IX as King 20 Mark

1606 Swedish King Charles IX - 1 Mark Silver coin - Standard Circulation - Image by Numista.com

1607 Stockholm Carl IX 4 Mark

you have seen from just the few images above, the ancient streets, the Royal Palaces, churches, art, statues, books, buildings, and various castles were filled with the name of the Creator.

Many countries also added the יהוה **YHWH (Yahweh)** on coins and medals. Medals were created for various reasons, such as commemorating battles won, weddings, or other celebrations. These coins and medals with the Tetragrammaton were created by people

1619 Coin - Netherlands

in Sweden, the Netherlands, Germany, Hungary, Indonesia, Italian, Portugal, Denmark, and Sweden. Some dynasties, like the Danish and Swedish kings of Stockholm, minted God's name on their coins as part of their monetary systems.

These pages are a peek into the world of coins and metals minted showcasing the Divine Name, יהוה **YHWH (Yahweh).**

1668 Swedish Eric XIV Coin

1644 Yahweh in Hebrew. King Christian IV of Denmark and Norway. Gold coin

1669 GERMAN coin - Tetragrammaton with rays descending - Bride and Groom marriage of Ernst's son Frederick and Magdalena Sybilla of Weissenfels

1653 German coin - The Tetragrammaton in the sky. The city of Hamburg with Elbe River, Boats, and Ships

1677 German coin with Tetragrammaton - Commemorating The European Banking Cities - Amsterdam, Hamberg, Nurnberg, Venice

COINS AND METALS

1745 Frankfurt Germany - Holy Roman Empire. Franz I. On the Imperial Coronation at Frankfurt.

Dexteratum Coin

1967 Netherlands, Gold Token, Moshe Dayan image from Numiscorner

Portugaleser-O-horz coin

Chapter
12

The Name Yahweh

> *"Sing unto God, sing praises to his name: extol him that rideth upon the heavens by his name YAH, and rejoice before him."*
> *~ Psalms 68:4 KJV*

WHAT'S IN A NAME

Commonly, we think of a name as a word or set of words by which a person is known, addressed, or referred to. But a name is much more than this. Names are an incredibly important part of our identity. They carry deep personal meaning that relates to one's uniqueness. They undoubtedly influence the way one is seen. Names also display one's cultural, familial, and historical connections.

Every name has a meaning, a reason it has been connected to something specific. The study of names is called onomastics or onomatology. In these studies, it has been revealed that names convey a sense of who we are and how others relate to us. Researchers have discovered that a name describes a person's character, influences one's personality, and could serve as a type of self-fulfilling prophecy about a person's nature. In some studies, researchers have found that a person's name might be related to their appearance later in life.

Names are so important that dictionaries have been created to find their meanings. Like any word in the dictionary, a person's name can be traced back to its original meaning. A Name Dictionary often provides an immediate answer to the name's meaning and etymology. Etymology means the name's root, where the name came from, and its original meaning. When researching names, we find that there is an important or special meaning hidden within each one.

A name's ancient and deeper meaning can speak to you. Studies suggest that your name can affect the amount of success you'll achieve in your career, love life, and even where you choose to live. A name is a powerful and consequential part of us that conveys and creates meaning. They reveal something about who we are, where we come from, and where we're headed.

Names are essential to relationships. A name connects one to one's identity and individuality. But a name also connects one to another. Therefore, knowing and using someone's name creates a bond and relationship with them. The worship of יהוה **YHWH (Yahweh)** is a foundational aspect of the faith of the Israelites. This belief is purely spiritual and not a religion. The ancient Israelite relationship with יהוה **YHWH (Yahweh)** was based on a sacred, everlasting bond called the Covenant. It was a kindred bond where they looked to יהוה **YHWH (Yahweh)** as Father, and יהוה **YHWH (Yahweh)** called Israel – son. Exodus 4:22: ***"And thou shalt say unto Pharaoh, Thus saith יהוה YHWH (Yahweh), Israel is my son, even my firstborn:"*** As time passed, this relationship between יהוה **YHWH (Yahweh)** and the Israelites influenced other religions, including the Jewish religion, and the beliefs of Christianity and even Islam.

Names are important. The first thing יהוה **YHWH (Yahweh)** did after creating man was to name man, Adam. Then, after naming Adam, יהוה **YHWH (Yahweh)** brought everything to Adam to see what he would call it.

> ***"And out of the ground the יהוה YHWH formed every beast of the field, and every fowl of the air; and brought them unto Adam to see what he would call them: and whatsoever Adam called every living creature, that was the name thereof."***
> ***~Genesis 2:19 KJV***

Adam named everything.

"And Adam gave names to all cattle, and to the fowl of the air, and to every beast of the field;" ~Genesis 2:20 KJV.

The Hebrews also viewed names with honor and significance. In ancient Israelite times, they knew the importance, value, and sometimes power connected with one's name. They understood that a name did more than connect us to our identity. The Israelites knew that a name carried power, responsibility, and blessings. Names were tied to the authority of the one who carried the name.

The Israelites respected names; even picking a name demonstrated importance and was considered an honorary process. For the Israelites, names convey and create meaning in one's life. Some names even carry hidden messages from יהוה **YHWH (Yahweh)**.

The first thing יהוה **YHWH (Yahweh)** did in the book of Genesis after creating man was to give this new creation the name - Adam. The names given by יהוה **YHWH (Yahweh)** were some of the most powerful.

- Abram's name was changed to Abraham.
- Sarai's name was changed to Sarah.
- Jacob's name was changed to Yisrael (Israel).

These powerful name changes followed a transformation or conversion of the person, meaning they had to have a different name from the one before their changes. Such changes prove that a name is a masterfully crafted, powerful reward bestowed justifiably and with merit on the recipient.

This statement is especially true when it comes to the Name יהוה **YHWH (Yahweh)**!

THE CLOSING

"And they said unto him, From a very far country thy servants are come because of the name of the YHWH thy God: for we have heard the fame of him, and all that he did in Egypt," ~ Joshua 9:9 KJV.

In the creative process, God named himself according to his nature. יהוה **YHWH (Yahweh)** – The Self-Existing One, the One Who Has Being, Who Has Life, and Who is Alive. At its core, "Yahweh" means "The Existing God, The Supreme Divine Being, I AM."

This signifies the real Being of God, his Self-Existence, and that He is the Being of all beings. It also denotes his eternity, immutability, constancy, and faithfulness in fulfilling his promises. This Name, יהוה **YHWH (Yahweh)**, includes all time, past, present, and the time to come. It means more than 'I Am what I Am' at present. It also means 'I Am what I Have Been,' and 'I Am what I Shall Be,' and 'Shall Be what I Am.'

THE RIGHT NAME

"A good name is rather to be chosen than great riches, and loving favour rather than silver and gold." ~ Proverbs 22:1 KJV

The Old Testament teaches that Moses first met the God of Israel in a burning Bush. The thought of speaking to God through a bush that burned with fire but was not consumed by the fire is amazing. It shows the power of the one working or creating this miracle. Yet when Moses was told to go to Pharaoh to release the children of Israel, Moses still needed God to answer one important question. He said that the children of Israel would be asking him questions. They will ask, who is this God of our forefathers, Abraham, Isaac, and Jacob? What is his name?

> *"And Moses said unto God, Behold, when I come unto the children of Israel, and shall say unto them, The God of your fathers hath sent me unto you; and they shall say to me, What is his name? what shall I say unto them?" Exodus 3:13 KJV*

From this Bible verse, you can see that Moses knew the name of the God of the Israelites was important. You can also see that Moses did not even know the name then. Sometime after Jacob Israel's and the twelve sons' deaths, their generations had again lost the knowledge of the name of their God. Therefore, יהוה **YHWH (Yahweh)** had to reintroduce himself to them through Moses when Moses asked what he should tell them.

> *"And God said unto Moses, I AM THAT I AM: and he said, Thus shalt thou say unto the children of Israel, I AM hath sent me unto you.*
>
> *And God said moreover unto Moses, Thus shalt thou say unto the children of Israel,* יהוה *YHWH (Yahweh) God of your fathers, the God of Abraham, the God of Isaac, and the God of Jacob, hath sent me unto you:* <u>this is my name for ever</u>, *and this is my memorial unto all generations." ~ Exodus 3:14-15 KJV*

Now, after reading this book, you too have been introduced or reintroduced to the name יהוה **YHWH (Yahweh)**, the God of the Hebrew Israelites, the God of the Bible, the God of Jesus, Yahshua, the creator of the heavens and earth, God of this World.

Knowing the name יהוה **YHWH (Yahweh)** is just the first step in your journey to bring yourself out of the cave of darkness into the light. The next step up is to research and study all you can find about יהוה **YHWH (Yahweh)**, what it means to exist, and the word God. The more you research and study the name יהוה **YHWH (Yahweh)**. The more you will raise yourself out of the darkness. Then, as you come out of darkness into the light of יהוה **YHWH (Yahweh)**, let the light within you shine so you can share this truth with others.

In this world of confusion, misinformation, and dishonesty, you must dig and research everything. It often seems impossible to know what is true and what is not true. There is no shortage of names for God. He is called by hundreds of different so-called names, attributes, or titles. However, only one stands alone, and that Name is יהוה **YHWH (Yahweh)**.

יהוה **YHWH (Yahweh)** is the covenant-keeping Name. God calls himself "יהוה **YHWH (Yahweh)**" when he first enters into the Covenant with Abraham. Entering into the Covenant means יהוה **YHWH (Yahweh)** taught Abraham the Truth about the Name.

It was also this Covenant that changed Abram's Name to Abraham and Sarai's Name to Sarah. Learning the knowledge and power of the Name יהוה **YHWH (Yahweh)** changed Abraham and Sarah into new beings.

It was important for Abraham, Sarah, and Israel to have the correct name, which reflected their new being and who they had become. Therefore, how much more important is יהוה **YHWH (Yahweh)**'s name?

Many people often say their prayers don't get answered when they pray. Maybe it is time to use God's correct name. If someone called you by an incorrect name and continued to call you by that name even when they were told your correct name, would you gladly adhere to their calls on you for services or needs? Most people would not.

Getting someone's name correct is a sign of respect. So know that this is the same respect that יהוה **YHWH (Yahweh)** deserves from you. Calling God by His personal name, יהוה **YHWH (Yahweh)** shows the reverence and respect deserving of Him.

Lastly, remember that covenant is another word for Truth, and יהוה **YHWH (Yahweh) is the covenant God. Therefore, it is only through the name** יהוה **YHWH**

(Yahweh) that truth is found. יהוה YHWH (Yahweh) is the true name of God. Now that you have learned this information. You have a responsibility. It is up to you to research and study everything you can find about the name יהוה YHWH (Yahweh). *You shall know the truth, and the truth will make you free. ~ John 8:32 KJV.* יהוה YHWH (Yahweh) is that name that helps to set you free. Freedom only comes through the knowledge of this truth.

"And be renewed in the spirit of your mind."
Ephesians 23:4 KJV

"Because I will publish the name of יהוה YHWH (Yahweh): ascribe ye greatness unto our God."
Deuteronomy 32:3

"Go ye therefore come and teach all nations, baptizing them in the name of יהוה YHWH (Yahweh):"
Matthew 28:19

"That all the people of the earth may know that יהוה YHWH (YAHWEH) is God, and that there is none else."
1Kings 8:60

Blessed be the name of יהוה YHWH (Yahweh) from this time forth and for evermore.
Psalms 113:2

REFERENCES

PRINT AND INTERNET

King James Version of the Bible

- Yahweh Bible by Crystal City Publishing
- Hebrew-Greek Key Study Bible
- Scofield Bible
- Dakes Annotated Bible

New Jerusalem Bible

King James Bible Online, https://www.kingjamesbibleonline.org

The Bible Gateway, https://www.biblegateway.com

Strong's Exhaustive Concordance, James Strong; Reference Print

Strong's Concordance with Hebrew and Greek Lexicon, online resource, https://www.eliyah.com/lexicon.html

Strong's Exhaustive Concordance, online resource, https://www.biblestudytools.com/concordances/strongs-exhaustive-concordance

Blue Letter Online Resource, https://www.blueletterbible.org/lexicon

Gesenius Hebrew and Chaldee Lexicon, Study Resource,

https://www.blueletterbible.org/study/lexica/gesenius/

Brown-Driver-Briggs Lexicon

The Eerdmans Bible Dictionary

Smith's Bible Dictionary

The Synonym Finder, JI Rodale

The Interpreter's Dictionary of the Bible, An Illustrated Encyclopedia

by Keith George, George Arthur Buttrick, George Arthur Buttrich

Online Etymology Dictionary

Online Dictionaries
- **Dictionary.com**
- **Merriam Webster**, https://www.merriam-webster.com

Wikipedia Free Encyclopedia, Genesis Flood Narrative, https://en.wikipedia.org/wiki/Genesis_flood_narrative#:~:text=Scholars%20believe%20that%20the%20flood,of%20the%202nd%20millennium%20BCE.

David Rolph Seely, "William Tyndale and the Language of At-one-ment," in The King James Bible and the Restoration, ed. Kent P. Jackson (Provo, UT: Religious Studies Center, Brigham Young University, 2011), 25–42

- Tyndale was the first to use the terms Jehovah, Passover, atonement, scapegoat, and mercy seat in his translation of the Old Testament.

Britannica, The Editors of Encyclopaedia. "Yahweh". Encyclopedia Britannica, 27 Jun. 2023, https://www.britannica.com/topic/Yahweh. Accessed 5 November 2023.

Mark, Joshua J. "Yahweh." World History Encyclopedia. World History Encyclopedia, 22 Oct 2018. Web. 04 Nov 2023.

Wikipedia - wikipedia.org/wiki/Yahweh

Wegner, Paul D., "The Journey from Texts to Translations: The Origin and Development of the Bible." Paperback, 1 August 2004

Yahweh Restoration Ministry - www.yrm.org

Abrahamic Study Hall, Mesha Stele, https://www.abrahamicstudyhall.org/2021/09/05/mesha-stele-the-oldest-inscription-about-tetragrammaton

Hall, Emily, "The Great Schism - What Is the Great Schism of 1054?" Bible Study Tools, 10 Jan 22 https://www.biblestudytools.com/bible-study/topical-studies/what-is-the-great-schism-of-1054.html#:~:text=The%20Great%20Schism%20of%201054%20resulted%20from%20a%20power%20struggle,and%20the%20Roman%20Catholic%20Church. 10 October 23.

Library of Congress - www.loc.gov

Jefferson National Parks Association, https://jnpa.blog/2023/05/23/the-unique-history-of-st-louis-first-church

Tetragrammaton – St. Mary's Church, Wivenhoe History, www.wivenhoehistory.org.uk

Louvre Bible - https://louvrebible.org.uk

Wikimedia Commons, Tetragrammaton in Christian art, https://commons.wikimedia.org/wiki/Category:Tetragrammaton_in_Christian_art

List of Tetragrammatons in Art in Austria. (2023, November 1). In Wikipedia. https://en.wikipedia.org/wiki/List_of_Tetragrammatons_in_art_in_Austria

"Amen Etymology, Translations & Usage." Study.com, 27 January 2023, study.com/academy/lesson/amen-overview-usage-facts.html

Britannica, The Editors of Encyclopaedia. "Yahweh". Encyclopedia Britannica, 6 Nov. 2023, https://www.britannica.com/topic/Yahweh. Accessed 11 November 2023.

Read the full article "Yahweh's Desert Origins" by Juan Manuel Tebes in the Fall 2022 issue of Biblical Archaeology Review.

EXTRA IMAGES

Cre8tive Minds

Denisgo

Tomertu

Scott Flaherty

Crisfotolux

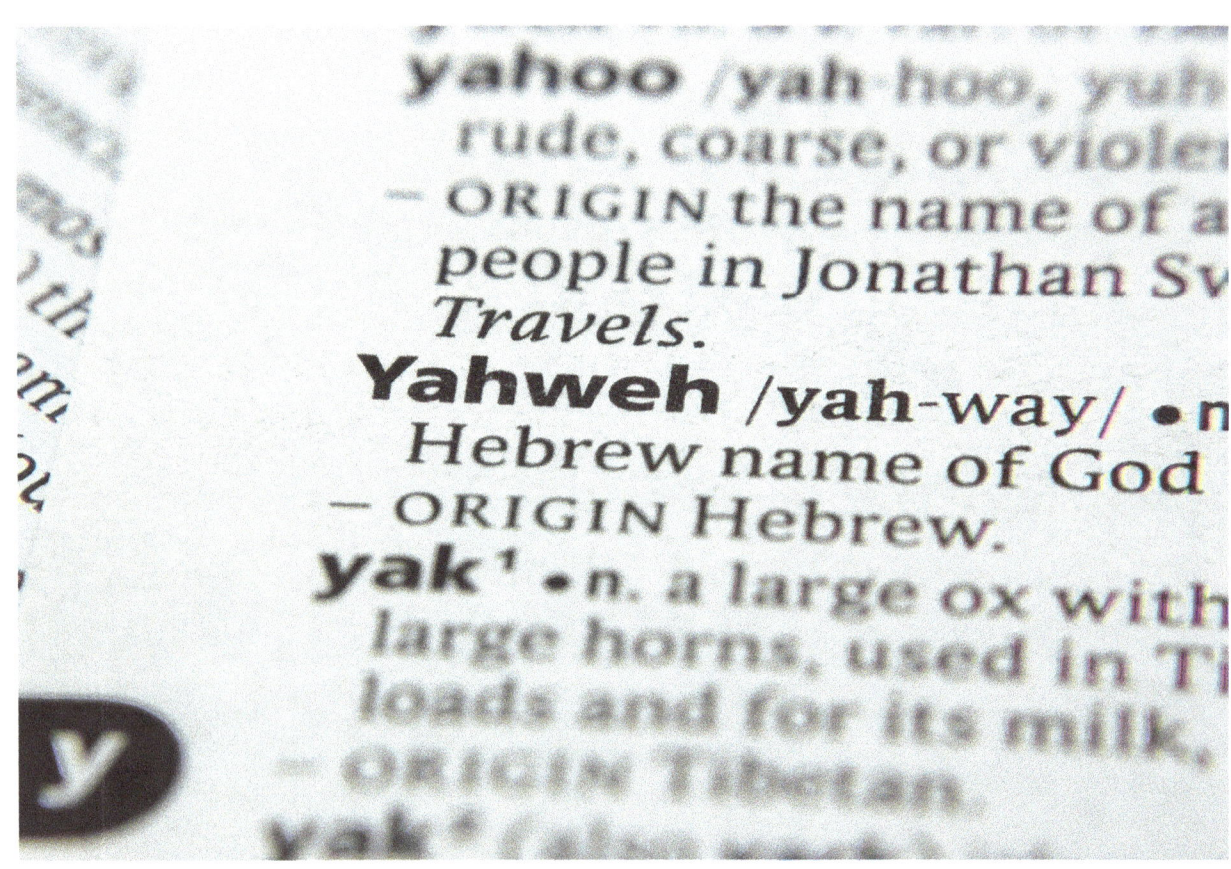

KOS Books
To learn about - The Kingdom of Shalom
Visit www.kingdomof shalom.com

www.ingramcontent.com/pod-product-compliance
Lightning Source LLC
Chambersburg PA
CBHW061404010526
44119CB00010B/258